Casting for the Cutthroat
& Other Poems

by Charles Entrekin

Berkeley Poets' Workshop & Press
Berkeley, California
1980

ACKNOWLEDGEMENTS

I want to thank the editors of the following publications in which some of the poems in this book first appeared: *Berkeley Poets Cooperative, West Branch, Aura, US1 Worksheets, Southern Poetry Review, Tunnel Road, Kudzu, Thunder City Broadsides, Bay Arts Review, California Living, Baltic Avenue Poetry Journal, The Smith, The Berkeley Poets Cooperative Anthology, 1970-1980.*

Also, Thunder City Press out of Birmingham, Alabama which first published a number of these poems in a chapbook, *Casting for the Cutthroat*, in 1977.

And the City of Oakland, California for "The People Poems" through which the poem, "Missoula Spring," first appeared as a poster on the BART (Bay Area Rapid Transit) trains in 1977.

And Yaddo Colony, Saratoga Springs, New York, for a grant which allowed me the space and time to think about these poems and the organization of this book.

And finally my friends and the members of the Berkeley Poets Cooperative whose support and criticism helped me more than they know – in particular Bruce Boston, Ramsay Bell, Marcia Falk, Bruce Hawkins, Alicia Ostriker, Rod Tulloss, and Jo Ann Ugolini.

Cover art – Maggie Entrekin

ISBN 0-917658-13-2

Typesetting by Eileen Ostrow
Printed at the West Coast Print Center, Berkeley, California

CONTENTS

FOREWORD

This is a book about the divisions I discover between the insides and the outsides of my world. Sometimes it seems to me I am so small a piece in this puzzle of my life that my heritage and my expectations outrun my capacity for sanity. And so I search for touchstones, for the places and the times when these divisions are healed, or if not healed at least become clear enough to be understood, in the way poems are understood.

Casting for the Cutthroat
& Other Poems

To a Child in the Rain

It was to play in the rain
you took off your clothes,
damned the gutter's river,
Red Mountain's water down Birmingham
streets, the way you could lie back
and be carried away, naked,
in the wet wash of summer rain,
and no plans but to swim down the river,
your street, become the world you lived in,
the fire tower and mountain top,
the mimosa and oak, as if the horizon
could reach down and touch you
like a sweeping brush stroke,
and you belonged to the landscape,
like sidewalk cracks and mud, the way
the tiny glass horses you held
remained rearing and alive
in their milky white light.

Yes

We were waiting in a stand of pines. The hounds announced themselves. Yes, he said, yes, they'll cross over there. And he began to run.

I remember catching up, my uncle taking the pistol from his clothes as he knelt on the road. It had rained earlier that morning and the smoke stayed close to the ground, the sound burning in my ears.

Yes, he said, fine rabbit if he doesn't have worms, and he smiled, his hand once again disappearing beneath his coat.

And the rabbit was so small, shot through the head, and I was amazed and puzzled, a child knowing that shot was a feat of perfection somehow. So small and he had shot it from so far away.

So small, and yes, he had stood there holding it by the ears, the wind bending around us, the trees singing the song of what could be remembered, but never again touched.

A Day's Work

For so little pay
to move all day with that weight
slung backwards and watch the dust
cover my hands like a new skin,
to stagger behind a black man who pulls
forward like a horse in harness,
so much power in his arms and back,
to lift that white substance from the plant,
that feeling of the seeds stuck in the center,
to stuff cotton balls in one smooth motion
without breaking stride
till it's sun-down beside the oak
beneath a red-varnished sky,
and an old man plopped down beside me,
wiping his eyes, face dust brown as mine,
saying, Damn wind done made me cry.

1941

Arriving in the parking lot
the evening I'm born, he stands
hands in his empty pockets,
fresh from a high school
that never taught him anything
about anything except fighting
and the war going on,
and knows that green sea of wall lockers
is behind him. It is August
and the black pavement still steams
with rain. Staring up
the high brick wall and windows
he tries to guess which one I'm in,
not yet believing there is one,
those square yellow lights like sleep
and a dream he can't wake up from.

Tone Poem

Inside the dream, light
turns the color of bone,
and knowing the right direction
a bird circles the nest,
a mons veneris, all
twigs with the leaves
and feathers packed
down inside,
and you have ceased
falling.

The Artist
for John Mullen

Everyone is an artist, he said,
inside. Inside there is someone
very, very old, someone only
an ancestor would recognize,
someone sheltered in a doorway
singing songs in a dew-dropping cold,
singing songs we always seem to know
as if we'd heard the words long, long ago.

Line Drawing: Self-Portrait

This man seems to have left
all his directions in a house
burned down in another life.
It's the puzzlement in his eyes,
mere circles of incompleted lines
complementing angles of the shoulders,
slim,
a man outside the joy of abandonment,
each line defined in the arc of another,
fingers closing into oval
over cigarette,
little finger extended,
the hand like a claw
grasping at what
has not been found.

Thoughts Stolen from Sleep

The snow on a branch in winter
and iron pipes wrapped against the cold,
these feelings are like sleeping while awake,
the selves you wrap up in, the thefts
you render smaller and smaller until
they begin to disappear, like small
lead bullets lodged in your heart,
no damage, no epiphany, only
a kind of icy clarity,
a metaphor that feeds upon itself,
the whole range of your experience,
the sound of it!

The Best of Friends
for Lee Fesperman

 In the East Bay mud
ride black rubber tires;
through tide after tide
they surface, glistening
with night's viscous reward
for wearing out.
 Long-eyed rodents
mount them in the dark
and wait the coming of dawn.
 Like someone playing
the piano, divertimento,
something ends,
can not be started again.

Grammar School Lesson
for Demian

Said, "Dad, could you help me a minute?"
your math book laid out on the table.
Nothing easier, percentages, fractions,
    but then your tears ruined
all my answers, thinking words like "exacerbate"
and "patience,"
    how events appear like conjugations of verbs:
wanting to help, needing to be helped,
hating of the helper, punishment of the helped.
    My life feels like an equation,
the way your hands are shaped
exactly like mine.

Thoughts from a Plane over Birmingham

My mother sick, the plane drifts
years, banking for landing, and suddenly
I'm home.
and the orange, industrialized sky
still says the furnaces are working overtime,
steel from the steel-born town.
The stewardess shakes the sleepers awake,
engines rev, landing gear down, and the home
I thought I'd left behind returns
as we touch the ground. Home
because what's free was never born,
because what opens at the beginning remains
open till the end.

Nightsong

     And what could be done
has been done to her. An acid rain
falls over New York; and as you sleep
a white, day-light moon seems to speak,
saying,
     take these dreams, shiny and bald
as they are, no expectations turn
as she turns.
     But no matter the words in your throat
you wake to a gray covered day, the whisper
of dawn rain, and it fills you with the sound
of weeping, with the sorrow that comes
when you don't know what's wrong.

The Art of Poetry

Once more, buddy, your last ride
has left you behind and nothing can be done.
You want someone to come, a silver angel,
to seize your hair and lift you from the earth.
But the weight of your two feet
presses against the ground. No one comes
to save you. It's too cold to stand still
and too dark to run.
Once more, buddy, you write
to save yourself. Here's the barn.
Here the horses are warm. Here, on a dark
night, between towns, between meals,
simply the heat of other animals is enough.

Line Drawings

1

Although it is you
the artist does not see you.
The line remains flat,
no more than surface,
a figure without shadow or depth.
Yet it is you;
that is your face
showing the uncertainty, your pose,
and the artist draws something
almost whole and defined
before giving up, before
the map of your bones
is forgotten, before the years
of his training take over.
His lines have their own reasons;
his hand pleasures in itself.

2

The way thought removes itself
in times of conflict, the line
remembers only line. Intention
disappears. The way she becomes
again, without clothes, a nude,
this woman, breasts tilted upward,
captured here in her attitude
of turning away from all of us
who might have known her,
hand draped over hip
in defiance and invitation,
yet giving up, as if the world
only imagined her, discovered
for the first time her face
and the guilt, the unseeing smile,
each line beginning her loosening shape,
her body spread out,
emptied and available.

In Birmingham
for Annie Newton-Allison

Grandma is home from the hospital.
They couldn't kill *her,* she says, the way
they killed her son, Bud. The dead are so many
and so far behind.
　　She remembers the Depression, how Bud
had done the work of ten, not because he was stronger,
but because he was smarter, never wasted a thing
in his life. Dead, too, her husband who always wore
starched shirts because there were no excuses
before God, and her children who hadn't survived
childhood. It's everything and yet it's nothing,
nearly blind from cataracts, who recalls
her own grandfather come home to die who wrote
strange songs and poems on the backs of paper bags,
worthless words and another mouth to feed.
　　Her mother was an ignorant woman, she says,
and asks if we know about the caves near Bridgeport.
There are bones there, she's heard, artifacts
that go back two thousand years. She says she remembers
Birmingham before the streets were paved. It's everything
and yet it's nothing. In the back yard she's had
a pecan planted to replace the fig. The tree
had worn itself out, she says; it had stopped
bearing fruit.

High, All-night Driving to Berkeley

Drink beer, follow the headlights,
the highway knows where a woman waits
who loves me. Drunks pass on by;
all maniacs stay in bed; I'm high
and Berkeley's near with its strong
ocean-like ways. The desert behind, a song
plays in my ear. Already sea waves run white
lines one at a time down the moon-lit night.
Your tides pull me along; your curve of thigh
runs in my mind; your round brown eyes
close once again. Take me, take me, says the song;
the maps show I can make no wrong
decisions. Home, to know your body as before;
I am a desert wrecked-dreamer come to shore.

Spring Letter to Donald Phelps
(with love and for your bad handwriting)

First opened your letter several days ago;
small tatters of words still fall out
unrecognized, and at night I feel presences,
predatory shapes at my window, and sad animals
hurt greatly, returning home in the dark.
It's in their eyes.
     Last evening I read it again, and again
could make out only the good parts. Comes clear
like some piece of news read thru blurred print,
yesterday's paper unwrapped from a fine trout dinner.
It's good. I trust you. Intuit what you say.
     This spring brings a drought they tell us
though it's rained two weeks straight; only a spring
rain, they say, too little too late. Even so
I feel afloat in a great gray, forever green
and foggy land. The drought seems only in the news.
     Living here makes me want to cry out
like an Aztec, "Hey! Lifegiver, how come you so shy?
Why don't you talk to us?"
     But it's spring and once again the business men
have returned from the slopes. Broken limbs.
Beautiful tans.
     Sometimes I feel I have no instincts here,
no voice for the absence of seasons. I want to hide
in alleyways, but soldiers hide there, eyes gone inward,
no legs; toss one a quarter and two old men rise
from garbage cans, strike at the silver color.
     Tonight I want only to hide on the dark side
of words, no need to understand, and flee
with the animals from some black shape
at home in this forever green land.

Crossing into Mexico

We come here as tourists
thinking of Aztecs in the interior
and discover the border towns,
houses made from Coca-Cola signs,
homes built from the scrap of an empire
next door.
    Here failure becomes real
in the uncurious outstretched hands
of children, where our cheap yellow Fiat
leaps like a coin in the sun.
    When we leave these towns
I think of Trotsky, the man with an axe
in his head, of Zapata and his silver white stallion,
but before us is the desert, a desert
that knows nothing of hope,
and I am almost grateful for the emptiness,
the illusory lakes rising and falling
over the highway.

Blackbirds Flying

Sometimes I discover myself here,
strangely awake and surprised
by the redwood in her backyard—
the way women walk from the hips down
and the men shamelessly watching,
calculating the measure of innocence
in the movement, the natural rhythm—
the way she never wakes as I slip out
down the highway, the car floating
along the hillsides, and the wind blowing me
only God knows where.

At Codornices Park
for Bruce Hawkins,
poet and Sunday morning guard

And when pores open, legs pumping,
I see that his court awareness still survives,
a forty-year-old four-eyes who understands
this language of fast breaks and finger-tip
finesse, the backdoor pass and give and go,
and easy lay-ups.
Because here is control
and that fun of full extension,
the face and flush of perfect
pick and roll. Because his hands
are filled with suggestions.
Because always his inscrutable sentences
begin in the arc of a hook shot.
And the ball falls, spinning backwards
a prescribed imagistic route,
a will creating its own reasons
for grinning: sunlight, trees,
this irrevocable letting go
of what is already falling,
that sense of sweetest swish
thru unbroken string.

Missoula Spring

     I have become
one of my own poems.
This morning the covered streets
opened black in melting snow.
     I was wrong.
Winter gone, a flower
opens in me, a song, words
crawl in my veins,
a carnation of the brain,
a dogwood.

This Stillness

As she goes up the stairs, suddenly
I remember a river I once watched
rushing powerful and dark after a long rain.
    Her shoulders seem thin and spare.
I stare at her thighs softly splotched
with white paint. Two canvases tonight.
Fatigue rests in her eyes. She says good night.
    Overhead a jet rumbles through the dark,
cars pass in the street. I listen as she undresses.
The children sleep. And I remember the river:
    how it seemed strangely unfamiliar, becoming
a remorseless, ceaseless roar, taking everything
within its reach; and I sat beside it on the bank, arms
around my knees, holding this stillness inside me.

Holding the Invisible

Meaning,
holding those things which can not be seen,
which I can not show you,
the way a vase tilts inside me
when you walk by,
the way we've lived in each other's lives
as if it made no difference,
a breath of air,
the wind in the curtains,
the way we come together in the dark,
that feeling of something falling,
my out-stretched hands.

The Disappearance of John

A young woman is working over her husband.
He's becoming a statue. She hammers away, shouting,
"John, John, I know you can hear me. John?"
        But even as she hammers, he's slipping
into stone. He is not escaping, he knows,
the blood is ceasing to flow, replaced
bit by bit by stone.
        Already his eyes appear to be fading,
that feverish glow of anxiety gone. "John?
Are you in there?" and the chisel in haste
placed just center of the shoulder blades,
"John?"
        Staring at the resultant dust
on her kitchen floor, she stamps her foot,
"John, this has gone too far!"
before she sweeps him up, and stores
what remains in a silver jar.

I pick you out, a man to become,
yes and no together; you lead me
into the desert. Your single words
are too thick for meaning. I
can't make them out. The cactus
plants are all I understand. And
the heat.
    In the moment I look around
you fall behind: whose death
do I feel? This is all a dream.
I wake, think of writing it down.
A man walks in through my window
from Montana. "Thirty white geese
are saved from extinction," he says,
helps himself to my liquor.
We ignore the snow.
    "I was just in Mexico," I said,
"did you feel something die?" He rages out
in the midst of a blizzard, with my liquor.
This is another dream. They flower
like carnations in a bowl. The white petals
all sink to the ground in a row.

In San Francisco

Coming towards me
like light from a distant star
not yet arrived anywhere
he entered the park
fondling an animal-headed
smooth-carved redwood cane;
    then pushing his black
leather jacket loose at the neck
his dark-skinned hand
found and placed the harp,
the black eyes closing,
the coffined chords
a hymn, a dirge,
    and suddenly I know how
the sounds of what I have broken
are healing in the ground.

Intonation

In the last of the daylight
the harbor opens like a door,
and jet black cormorants
bloom from the boat.
I feel frightened by their flight,
as if things are not what they seem,
something changing inside me,
a dream, words falling in my throat.
Wing and wing we are peeling
toward gulls. The sun is failing
in an acid haze. We move with a host
of fiberglass boats, the deep water bells
like someone calling.

All Those Women Wanting to Die

No longer takes me by surprise.
     The heavy magic of dreamers
sometimes self-destructs; only their words
are left behind. The body floats away,
     a black coach in January air, a wind
over coastal mountains, returning home,
zephyrs, ciphers,
     like frail shadows
before the light goes out.

The Photograph Is Wrong

for Janice K.

It was on a chert-red road near Birmingham,
our weathered gray farm house tilting
toward the earth. Green fingers of kudzu
had claimed the chimney and roof.
    When I look closely I can make out
railroad beds and a field of dead grass
in the distance. It was taken in Indian summer.
You are sitting under the mimosa trees, looking
like life has been good to you. It wasn't true.
    That was the year it snowed, a false spring
bloom on everything. I remember pointing to the trees,
saying how beautiful they were, undressed that way
and standing in ice.

Advantage

In France beside some shabby old wall
the water runs dirty with sunlight
and I walk, moss-brown stones beneath my feet,
toward you with open arms. You are blond now.
You have changed only the color of your hair.
All the rest remains the same.
    In your eyes I see you don't understand,
as if you're puzzled by my greeting. Being polite
you invite me to coffee before finding you're afraid:
there are no witnesses. Always we are alone.
It's then you begin to doubt, and I discover
once again how your grave face will unravel,
    remembering when we were young,
when your dark hair glistened like a river in the sun.

Carpé Diem
for Maggie in Berkeley

You can't find your shoes.
    Exiting your closet as from the insides
of a civilization you stand in the ruins:
all the etcetera of a lifetime: your huge
Black cadillac of a baby carriage, slide
projector, vacuum cleaner, umbrella . . .
    but not the shoes you need.
    You enter the bathroom without looking back,
slip into a hot tub of water. Your eyes seethe
brown with wickedness over your body. The suds
have crept to your hair.
    With a breath, your breasts float high
in the gray water.
    You are alive.
    You become, slowly, the woman's body
you understand, your own, and
    you know when you step from the tub,
wet and warm-red, with
      pieces of dreams still molten inside you,
      how porcelain your world can become.

Objet D'Art

In the beginning
there was a feeling of being found,
discovered,
the way he fit so neatly inside her
world view of things,
his appearance as it were,
and the armature of his being
becoming by necessity the base
which best displayed her beauty
so alarmingly.

Dream of Leaving You

This dream about leaving you
begins with your clothes on the floor
and flowers falling from your hair;

then there's an icy drink
at my elbow and the air
of a conversation that will not end,

the way time sits in your mouth
like cold sunshine and doors
wink open around you.

Angel Island

On the ferry deck, facing Tiburon and
Belvedere, you remember a man who once lived here
who told you his therapist had him lie naked
on a four-poster bed, and screamed his sorrows
into a sound-proofed room. But leaving the dock
the wind covers your thoughts, and nothing remains
but the Bay and the gay clinking of easy
conversations, a holiday.
      For two hours you track back through trees
to discover the barracks and bomb shelters,
that lingering feeling of Yale graduates in knickers
and argyle socks, and then the sudden gulls
when land sheers into bay.
      And here, next to the wispy white clouds
and the Golden Gate, it becomes clear how context
is everything, how the ocean has shaped this place
every hour of its existence, how even the deer come
down from the mountain sides, begging food, to fidget
beside a ball game, the way they've grown fat
without enemies, become the ghosts of dead soldiers,
the way they move, trapped and frightened, yet tame,
like something haunting that lives inside you,
that exposed feeling of submarine nets, of shuttered
barracks, of a peace that hides a sleeping war.

Point Reyes Station

I stand at land's edge,
fat buds barely
breaking into green, and
suddenly there's no sun,
no Alabama breeze,
only the Pacific cold mists
and this rising and falling
inside me, this longing
for roots, for no fear
of the forever false spring
which surrounds me.

April at Yaddo

This morning, nearly dawn
I wake suddenly, alone
in a strange house vain
with the ghosts of writers.

Slowly the dark lifts
and with it the thought
of your shoulders and back,
you, asleep beside me.

A bird stirs the patches of snow;
your body slips out across the continent.
Strange, how we never seem to know
the ways we own one another.

Three Evenings

I. Snow lies along the edge
of the road, peeled away
like birch-bark parchment.

I try to tell you
only what's on my mind,
but my words have no sound
on their own, and the cold
settles in the corners
of the house.

II. It has begun to rain.
The drain rattles with water
to the ground. I sit at the window,
watch the pines bend with the wind,
the snow as it begins to sink.

Only one voice refuses to give in;
I listen as a crow calls
and calls again.

III. This evening there is sunlight
in the pine straw and a heavy,
whispery breeze on the hilltops.
Everything feels emptied.

There is nothing to say.
Decisions are like aspens and birch,
speaking when no one's listening.

Crazy Lady

Only dreams and sweet revenge from a soft
romance – someone stole her baby. Dilated
eyes now search your face. Was it you?
A judge declared it best, and so look,
here's to elegance and extravagance
and her tough beauty on the streets.

    But today she's not high enough;
she feels the parenthesis of her sex
closing over emptiness. She moves
to hold you fast, poised at the edge
of herself. You have to make everything
simple, she says; align things by ones
before you divide.

    But touch no more than her
thin bare arms and a light
comes on inside her, and then a toast,
here's to her Byzantine beauty, and a home
away from home, sweet San Francisco,
here's to where she sleeps in the streets,
and her mouthtalker, eyeseer poetry.

The Witness

The need for perfection and
the mounting failures
and distractions
fill your clothes, yet
like the witness in poetry
reporting on what was seen,
nothing more,
the song, the rhythm, the plot,
and nothing more, you see
only the vision and,
like the reason for eating,
feel it
necessary,
living.

Casting for the Cutthroat

He sneaks after some woman who could not love him,
a woman from his school days, who would never love him.
He knew it, sneaking like a thief after the praise
from her lips, like a fisherman casting
only for the cutthroat, living
out his years forever dumb
before this woman who could touch him,
thinking only the barrenness of Garnet,
Montana could cure him,
this madness that could not be cured,
his own special madness,
the way the green of a river bank
reminds him of her,
the way she's always young as porcelain
and he's grown old, his books
like school houses ablaze in the snow.

Charles Entrekin was born and raised in Birmingham, Alabama. He took his B.A. in English from Birmingham Southern College, was a graduate student in Philosophy at Vanderbilt University and the University of Alabama, and completed his M.F.A. in Creative Writing at the University of Montana. One of the founders of the Berkeley Poets Cooperative, he has also taught at various colleges and universities, worked as a Consultant in the field of Computer Science, and served as the Associate Director of the Center For Contemporary Writing at John F. Kennedy University, Orinda, California. This is his third book of poems.

BOOKS FROM BPW & P

Jackbird by Bruce Boston, fiction, 88 pages, $2.00

Slow Juggling by Karen Brodine, poetry, 48 pages, $2.50

All Pieces of a Legacy by Charles Entrekin, fiction & poetry, 54 pages, $2.50

Once More out of Darkness by Alicia Ostriker, poetry, 32 pages, $2.00

Wordrows by Bruce Hawkins, poetry, 40 pages, $2.00

Over by the Caves by Jennifer Stone, fiction, 64 pages, $2.50

Snake Blossoms by Belden, fiction & poetry, 64 pages, $2.50

Seaward by Betty Coon, poetry, 44 pages, $2.50

Half a Bottle of Catsup by Ted Fleischman, poetry, 40 pages, $3.50

Wash Me On Home, Mama by Peter Najarian, fiction, 84 pages, $2.50

Newspaper Storeis and Other Poems by Pat Dienstfry, poetry, 36 pages, $3.75

Berkeley Poets' Cooperative Anthology, 1970-1980, 256 pages, $6.95

BPW & P
P.O. Box 459
Berkeley, Ca. 94701